STEPHANIE MAY WILSON

THE
Lipstick Gospel
PRAYER JOURNAL

How to Talk to God Like
He's Your Best Friend

Stephanie May Wilson

PUBLISHED BY ANTHEM WORKSHOP
ANTHEMWORKSHOP.COM

Introduction

Does prayer ever feel tricky to you? It definitely does for me.

Whether you've never prayed, haven't prayed recently, or you've been praying all your life, prayer can be a confusing thing. It's a bit like hope, or joy, or folding a fitted sheet—it's one of those things that's hard to pin down, hard to master—it's hard to know if you're doing it right.

Some of us are new to prayer—we've never been taught how; we don't have a clue how to begin.

Some of us have been praying all our lives, which sometimes leaves our prayer lives feeling a bit stale.

Some of us use big words when we pray—all "thees" and "thous." God is so big and holy and powerful; we feel like we have to perform if we're going to talk to a God like that.

Some of us avoid prayer altogether because it just feels too hard, too weird, or we feel unworthy of approaching God when we've made such a mess of things.

Some of us are at a great place when it comes to our prayer lives; we just want more. We want to experience more of Him; we want to see Him do bigger things in our lives; we want to go deeper.

And I think that no matter how much we've prayed, or haven't prayed—no matter how long we've been a Christian—that's why we're all here. We all want to know God better, and that's just perfect because that's exactly what this prayer journal is all about.

It's always been amazing to me how God is so many things all at once. He's powerful and holy. He's not to be taken lightly. But He's also tender, and close, and wants to really know us; He wants to have a relationship with us. Isn't that amazing?

And the thing I've discovered about relationships is that the more time we spend together, and the more we open up to each other about our lives, the closer we feel. I've discovered this to be true with God too.

The more time I spend with Him, and the more I open up to Him about the best, and hardest, and silliest, and messiest parts of my life, the closer I feel to Him—just like with my best friends.

So that's how I've started to pray over the years. Each morning I wake up and spend some time with God. I read a devotional, read the Bible for a little bit, and then I take some time to pray. And, as I pray, I talk to God like I do my best friends, sharing the truth about what's going on in my heart and in my life, not in fancy language, but honestly. And it's changed everything.

During this time over the last several years, God has become my very best friend. He's been the first one to hear about my joys and my greatest sorrows. He's been the one to listen as I've talked endlessly about decisions, and relationships, and jobs, and friends. We're in this together, God and I, and I've found there's nothing sweeter in the whole entire world.

So whether you've known Him all your life, or are getting to know Him for the very first time, this 90-day prayer journal is a practical way of going deeper in your relationship with God. The daily prompts will help you to curl up and spend time with Him—telling Him about your life, your hopes, your dreams, and your fears—the things you find to be lovely, and hard, and really, really funny.

More than ever before, we're getting to know the God who created the heavens and the earth, the God who is big and sweeping and powerful and majestic. But we're also getting to know the God who wants to become our very best friend. He's become mine, and I know He wants to become yours too.

That's what we're doing in this prayer journal over the next 90 days. God has so much in store for us, and I can't wait to get started. You ready? Let's begin!

Talk to God about your relationship with Him. Are there things about your relationship you wish were different, better, or closer? If so, talk to Him about it, and don't be afraid to ask for His help. "God, please help me get closer to you, please help me love you better," is a wonderful prayer to pray—and I can't think of a prayer God would rather answer!

God, I wish I knew you better. I wish I believed all the things you say are true about me. Can you help me do that? I want you at the center of all parts of my life and to feel your love and know your word. I wish I wasn't so scared to talk about you to others and share your message.

I feel like I hate myself. There is so much wrong with me + I always screw up everything. Am I going to screw up this job, this relationship, this life? I feel like Ive already failed. Have I failed you?

My hand is tired, and so am I, but I think tonight could maybe be a good start.

What do you have going on in your life these days? Tell God about it. Our prayers don't have to be formulaic, or formal at all. Update God on your life like you would a friend—"This is what is going on, this is what I'm working on, this is what I have coming up." God wants to be a part of our lives—the big, sweeping, scary parts, sure—but also the small, regular, everyday parts. Tell Him about those parts today. I know He can't wait to hear!

Hi God. Life is crazy these days! Work is slow right now so lots of projects. There's kind of some tension within the team right now, can you help with that? Help them to have understanding and empathy? And me too! lol

Cam and I are great - thank you for him. I see you working through him ☺ I pray you would maybe send him some love + encouragement today. And maybe keep him around a while? ♡

Shelby is in quaranteen (bad spelling) and I miss her sooo much! I can't wait to see + squeeze her Monday! Please can you help her to have a safe surgery + fast recovery? Also please help her to be safe in this new relationship? I'm worried about it/her. Will you reach out to her?

Last - The family moves tomorrow. Trying to block it out because I am scared and sad. Im going to miss them so much. I'll need your help and strength to get through. Can I lean on you please?

Feeling much better than yesterday, Still with a tired hand. lol. I hope we have a great Friday.

With love,

Amen

We talk to God more than ever when things are hard and scary, but He wants to be part of the beautiful, happy things in our lives as well. So with that in mind, what's something that's been bringing you joy lately?

My home! I love my apartment. It is such a sanctuary for me. Decorating for Christmas has been so fun.

Also my friendship with Shelby. She brings so much joy & love into my life. I feel very at peace around her.

Day 4

What are you worried about these days? Tell God about those things and invite Him into them. Ask Him to help you with them, and don't be afraid to be specific. If you are worried about paying a bill, ask God to help you. If you're upset about a broken relationship, ask God to help you mend it. 1 Peter 5:7 says, "Cast your anxieties on Him because He cares for you." So do that this morning. Gather up your worries, and hand them over to God by telling Him about them, and rest assured that He can and WILL help you through them.

Day 5

What's something that's happened in the last few days that's reminded you that God is good? Tell Him what it was, and thank Him for it, too!

Take some time to pray for the people in your life. If there's anyone who's going through something hard, or is sick, or is in a big transition, or is trying to answer a big question—ask God to help him or her today. The thing I always have to remember is that God loves my loved ones infinitely more than I do. Not only that, but prayer is truly the most helpful thing we can do for them. So pray for your people today.

Body image is such a hard thing for us as women. Feeling comfortable, confident, and beautiful in our skin is something we all want, but it's often so hard for us to get there. This morning, tell God about how you feel in your skin these days—if you feel beautiful, tell him! If you don't, ask Him to help you see and appreciate your body for how beautiful it truly is.

James 1:17 says, "Every good and perfect gift is from above, coming down from the Father of the heavenly lights, who does not change like shifting shadows." I just love that. What's one gift you've seen from God this week? It can be as big as grace or forgiveness or a new house or a baby being born, or as small as a really great cup of coffee. Every good and perfect gift is from above, so thank Him for one of them today.

What are some things you feel insecure about either in yourself or your life? Take some time to talk with God about them this morning. The beautiful thing about a relationship with God is that He not only wants to hear about the real, true things that are going on in our hearts and our lives, but He can also help us work through them in a way nobody else can! So bravely share about those insecurities this morning and ask God to free you from them.

Take some time this morning to tell God about your job or, if you're in school, tell Him about that! Tell Him about the good parts, the parts you enjoy, the parts that are going well, and thank Him for those. Also, take some time to tell Him about the hard parts, and ask for His help. God cares about your work life and your education. He's on your team!

There's nothing you could do to make God love you more, and there's nothing you could do to make God love you less. God loves you because He loves you because He loves you because that's who God is. That's the beauty of the Gospel. It's that amazing, and that hard to fully absorb. (Is that just me?) Ask God to help you understand those truths in new and deeper ways today.

Day 12

What is God teaching you these days? How is He growing you and changing you? If you're not sure, think of some areas where you might be struggling a bit. You know you want to be more this or less that, but you're not quite there yet. Or you're learning something but haven't quite mastered it. You're working through something, but you don't feel like you're all the way on the other side yet. Talk to God about how He's growing you and changing you today. Thank Him for helping you become the woman He created you to be.

We all have hard relationships in our lives—people we're not getting along with, people who are hard for us to love, relationships that feel broken, sometimes beyond repair. Talk to God about any difficult relationships you have in your life today, and ask Him for His help in them. God can bring healing and restoration to even the most broken relationships; He can in yours too!

Are there any habits in your life that you want to break—anything you tend to do that you just don't want to do anymore? Talk to God about it, and ask for His help. He's in this with you!

Our relationships with God can be serious and weighty at times, but they don't always have to be. Today, tell God about two fun things that are going on in your life these days. If you're in a particularly hard spot in life, it might be hard to think of two things, but I want you to try. Even in hard seasons, our lives are full of really great, really beautiful, and even really fun things. They're just sometimes harder to see. But when we take the time to look for them, they remind us of the goodness that still fills our lives. So take some time to reflect on two fun things you have going on in your life these days, and tell God about them.

Day 16

Are you feeling guilty about anything these days? When we do something we think might be wrong, we're so tempted to hide from God. But hiding never actually helps. Instead, when we can be up-front with God about what happened, confessing it to Him, and asking for His help, it helps us get through whatever the thing is; it helps us live a better way, and it also brings us closer to Him. Shame is never from God, and having an honest conversation with Him is the perfect way to get rid of it. So do that today! Talk to God about anything that's making you feel guilty; be honest about it, confess it, invite Him into it. Ask Him to forgive you, and to help you live a better way. He'll do it. I know He will.

Take some time to pray for our country, for anything you know is going on right now. The world can feel big and hard and messy so often, so outside of our control. But we can rest assured that God is in it all, and bigger than it all. So today, pray for the things going on in our country and ask God for His help in them.

Day 18

Where do you need God's help today? Tell Him about it and ask for the help you need. He's in this with you. You can count on Him. Also, leave a little bit of space at the end where you can write down how He showed up. Seeing our prayers prayed and then answered builds up our faith the way almost nothing else does. It'll be a reminder from your own life that God is there, and that when we pray, He answers!

What's a dream you have for your life? Every time I've told God about one of my dreams and invited Him into it, it's become something bigger and more beautiful than I ever could have come up with on my own. So share that dream with Him this morning and invite Him into it.

Day 20

Tell God about something beautiful that's happening in your life these days. It can be big, or small, or somewhere in between. God wants to hear about all the parts of our lives, the hard ones, and the lovely ones too.

Are there any things in your life, either in the present or the past, that you're ashamed of? It feels hard to talk to God about these things, but they're actually His specialty. There's nothing in the world that's too big for God to forgive, nothing too broken for Him to heal, and nothing that reaches beyond His ability to bring reconciliation and restoration. So talk to Him about those things this morning. Ask Him to make those areas of your life new. He's faithful. He'll do it. I promise, and even better, so does He!

Day 22

What's going on in your life this week? Tell God about it, and ask Him to help you in any areas where you need it!

Day 23

What's happening in the world that just breaks your heart? Maybe it's something going on in a certain country, or something happening to a particular group of people. Maybe it's poverty, or injustice, or war. Pray for that problem or for that group of people this morning, and brainstorm together with God some ways you can get involved and help!

Day 24

God loves you, He isn't disappointed in you, He isn't mad at you, and you haven't failed Him. He just simply loves you, absolutely, no matter what. That's hard to receive sometimes, isn't it? Talk to Him about how that truth makes you feel. And ask Him to help you understand it more fully today.

Day 25

What does your life look like these days when it comes to friendship and community? Tell God about it. If you have a wonderful community, thank God for it, and pray for your people today. Do you wish you had deeper friendships? A closer community? Ask God for opportunities to meet more people, and ask Him for the courage to pursue them.

Day 26

Is there anything in your life right now that feels intimidating? Tell God about it, and ask Him to help you break through that intimidation, to face whatever it is with courage and boldness.

Day 27

Whenever something beautiful or funny or lovely crosses my path, I feel like it's a little gift from God just reminding me that He loves me. Tell God about something that made you smile this week, and thank Him for the little reminder that He loves you. Because it's true, He really does.

What is something you've learned from a friend recently? I learn so much from my girlfriends every time I'm with them. Whatever it is, tell God about it this morning.

Every once in a while I have days where I have a hard time loving myself, and on my very worst days I am my own cruelest critic. But the good news is that, while we may be critical of ourselves, God isn't. That's not how He sees us. So spend some time talking to Him today about how you see yourself. Then ask Him to help you see yourself the way He sees you. He will help you; I know He will.

Take some time this morning to tell God about your family. Tell Him about the good parts, and thank Him for the ways your family is a gift. Also, tell Him about the hard parts and ask for His help with them. God cares about your family even more than you do. He also knows that family dynamics can be tricky, and even tremendously painful. So ask Him to help you with your family, in whatever way you need it today.

Every single part of our lives is better when God is in them. He brings color, life, true peace, real joy. Are there any corners of your life that feel like God isn't in them? Invite Him in today!

Day 32

What's something you love about your life these days? Tell God about it and thank Him for it!

Is there anything you think might be standing between you and God? Every once in awhile in my life there's something I know is keeping me away from God. It changes based on the season. Sometimes it's something that keeps me busy and distracted. Sometimes it's a messy thing in my life or a bad choice I'm consistently making. God isn't angry at us; He doesn't push us away when we have these things in our lives. But sometimes when we are holding onto them too tightly, I think we feel further away from Him. We can trust that if God is bringing something to mind that you might need to step away from for awhile, it's because life will actually be better if you do. So talk to Him about this today.

In Matthew 11:28 Jesus says, "Come to me, all you who are weary and burdened, and I will give you rest." So do that today. Talk to God about the places where you're weary, the areas of your life where you need rest or rejuvenation, and ask Him to give you those things today.

Day 35

Are there any mountains in your life right now? Anything that just feels too big to overcome? God's specialty is making a way when there isn't one, doing the impossible, helping ordinary people overcome insurmountable odds. So tell Him about your mountain today, and ask Him to help you overcome it.

Day 36

Psalm 139 says that we are perfectly and wonderfully made. But my gosh, isn't it hard to see ourselves that way sometimes? But that's who God says we are. That's what He says about us, and this morning, I want us to practice believing Him. Take some time and tell God three things you love about yourself. It might be easy; I hope it is! But just in case it isn't, I'm challenging you to stay in the conversation until you can come up with three. There are a thousand to pick from, I know it. You can do this!

Day 37

What are you afraid of today? Perfect love casts out fear. So talk to God about it, and ask Him to help you believe His truth instead of the voice of your fears.

God loves you TREMENDOUSLY, ENDLESSLY, no matter what! Spend some time talking to Him about that, and ask Him to help you understand that truth all over again today.

Day 39

What was the last thing that made you cry? Tell God about that today.

Day 40

What does your love life look like these days? Maybe you're single and loving it, or single and wishing this season would end—and fast. Or maybe you're dating someone and trying to figure out if they're the one. Or maybe you're engaged or married. Tell God where you are in your relationships these days. Thank Him for the parts that are good and wonderful, and ask for help in any areas where you need it.

What's something in life that you've wanted to try, but that makes you nervous? Tell God about it, and then ask Him to help you be strong and courageous. (And check out Joshua 1:9 for some encouragement along the way!)

Day 42

What are three things you're grateful for today? Spend some time reflecting and then thank God for them. When we focus on the things God is doing, on the good things we have and the ways He's providing, it helps us see Him in our lives more and more. God is so good and takes such good care of us. Take some time to notice and thank Him for it today.

Day 43

Are there any mistakes you've made that make you feel like you're disqualified from God being good in your life—an area where you think that God might have had a good plan for you, but you've certainly messed it up? Sweet friend, this just isn't true. Spend some time reading Romans 8:37-39 and talk to God about it. Nothing, nothing, nothing in the whole world can disqualify you from His love. That's the beauty of the Gospel.

Are there any areas of your life that are just plain hard right now? Ask God for a ray of hope in it, ask Him for some sunshine, and keep an eye out for it. You can trust Him to do that!

Day 45

What has God been doing in your friends' or family's lives recently? How has He showed up for them? How has He provided? I love seeing God do amazing things in the lives of my loved ones because it's such a great reminder that He can do the same for me. So spend some time talking to God about what you've seen Him do lately. Thank Him for the fact that He's faithful—in their lives, and in yours too.

Day 46

Is there anything about yourself you wish you could change? Maybe it's a tendency toward anger, or impatience, or jealousy, or fear. Talk to God about it this morning and ask for His help. God can absolutely set you free from those things, so start that conversation today.

Day 47

Is there something in your life that you really want, but still don't have? Tell God about it. God absolutely answers our prayers and, if He doesn't answer in the way we're hoping He will, or in the timing we're hoping for, it's because He has something better for us. So take some time to tell Him what you want in life, but don't forget to leave room for the fact that He might have something even better.

Day 48

Take some time today to pray for our world. Pray for any big things (or small things!) that you know are going on in other countries. Maybe you heard about them on the news, or from your favorite non-profit, or maybe you have loved ones in other countries that are being impacted. Prayer is powerful and effective and actually changes things, so pray for our world today.

Day 49

What's something you found really fun or funny recently? Tell God about it this morning!

Day 50

Is there something in your life that you know isn't good for you, but that you're having a hard time letting go of? Tell God about it this morning and ask Him to help you. I know He will.

Is there anything that makes you feel not good enough or unworthy of love? Talk to God about it, and then write yourself a short note with what you think He might say in response.

What are three things you're grateful for today? Tell God about them and thank Him for them.

Tell God about your current living situation. What are some great things about it? Thank Him for the ways He's taken care of you in this. What are some hard things about it? Ask Him for help in those areas.

Is there something in your life that you feel like God is asking you to do? If so, talk to Him about it. Ask Him to open up a door for you, and for the courage to help you walk through it. If nothing comes to mind, ask Him. Pray and ask Him if there's anything He wants you to be doing these days, any way you can get closer to Him or participate in the amazing things He's doing in the world, and ask Him to open up a door so you can get started.

Song of Solomon 4:7 says, "You are altogether beautiful, my darling; there is no flaw in you." That is how God sees you. Spend some time this morning telling God how this makes you feel, and ask Him to help you see yourself this way too.

Our prayers don't have to be fancy. In fact, Jesus says they shouldn't be. Tell God something honest and true today.

Are there any areas of your past that feel broken or unresolved? Ask God to meet you in those—to bring healing, forgiveness, restoration, and redemption.

Are there any areas of your life where you're having a hard time feeling content? Talk to God about that today and ask for His help.

Are there any people in your life who don't know God, but you really wish they did? Spend some time praying for them today. I am proof that God answers those prayers in incredible ways. Pray for your people today. He's listening.

Day 60

Are there any areas of your life where you aren't trusting God? Talk to Him about that today.

Day 61

How has God been taking good care of you lately? Take some time to reflect on that, to remember, and to thank Him for those things this morning.

Day 62

What's one thing you love about yourself? Thank God for making you truly good enough.

One of my all-time favorite verses is Romans 8:28. It's the verse I stand on when it feels like everything else is crashing down. It says, "And we know that in all things God works for the good of those who love him, who have been called according to his purpose." How have you seen God keep this promise in your life?

What's something that has you worried these days? Write it down, and tell God (and yourself!) that you're giving those things back to Him. God has this under control. He really does.

Are there any areas of your life where you feel like you're either too much or not enough? Talk to God about that this morning. (Spoiler alert: You're neither!)

Day 66

Take some time to tell God how much you love Him and to thank Him for who He is in your life.

What's going on in your life this week? Tell God about it, and ask Him to help you in any areas where you need it.

Is there someone in your life that's hurt you, someone you're angry at, or even someone you hate? Pray for them today. It's so hard, it feels so unnatural, but praying for our enemies unlocks something in our heart. Praying for them doesn't make what they did right or okay. It's not about that. It's about the fact that anger and resentment are heavy things to carry, and praying for them sets us free.

Day 69

If God were to write a love letter to you today, what do you think it would say? You may want to say, "I don't know! I have no idea!" but give it a try. If you get stuck, take a few minutes to remember what you know about God, and what you know God says about you. You can do this! I know you can!

Day 70

What was going on in your life this time a year ago? How has God shown up since then? How has He provided, changed things, changed you? Take some time to remember together, and then thank Him for all He's done.

Take some time to pray for your people today. Prayer is the very best thing you can do to help them with whatever it is they're going through. So ask God to help them and remember that God loves your loved ones better than you ever can and more than you ever will. So pray for your people today.

Day 72

What are some things you're hoping will happen in your future? Talk to God about those things, and ask Him for guidance and help as you walk in that direction.

God is all around us. His fingerprints, evidence of His love, they're everywhere. But sometimes He feels hard to find. Have you ever felt that way? Ask Him for help with that today. Ask Him to help you see Him in your day.

Day 74

What are three things that are making you smile today? Tell God about them! I know He wants to hear.

Talk to God about where you are in your church life today. Maybe you have a great faith community. If so, spend some time thanking God for it. Maybe you are having a hard time with your church these days, or haven't found a church where you feel like you belong. Or maybe you've been hurt by the church, or have never been a part of one. Wherever you are, talk to God about that this morning.

What do you need more of in your life these days? Joy? Peace? Patience? Guidance? Tell God about the situation this morning and ask Him for what you need. He'll provide. I promise and (even better!) so does He!

Are there any areas of your life that could be fuller and richer if God was involved in them? Talk to Him about those areas, and hand them over to Him this morning. Oh, and don't forget to keep an eye out for what He does in them. God writes better stories in our lives than we can, every single time.

Is there anything you're confused about, or even angry at God about? I think we all have these things. God is so good, but the world is so hard, and sometimes it's hard to reconcile the two. Talk to God about that. Just like any other relationship, when there are unspoken hurt feelings, distance grows between us. So close that gap by being really honest. Be mad if you want, tell Him how you really feel. Don't try to hide it. Trust me, He can take it, and you'll feel much closer to Him when you're done.

Day 79

What was going on in your life this time five years ago? How has God shown up in your life since then, how is your life different than it was then? How has He provided, changed things, changed you? Thank Him for that!

Are there any ways you feel like you've messed up today, or yesterday, or this week? Tell God about them, and then ask Him for forgiveness and to help you use that situation to grow. Then let yourself off the hook. We can't punish ourselves for something God isn't even punishing us for. He has forgiven you. Don't forget to forgive yourself too.

What are you looking forward to in life these days? Maybe you have a vacation coming up, or you're about to finish a semester at school. Maybe your family is coming to visit, or you have tickets to a concert you're excited about. Tell God about that this morning.

What's causing you stress today? Talk to God about it. Then write whatever it is down on a piece of paper, fold it up, and put it in your Bible or another safe place. There's no magic to this; it's just a physical representation of the fact that we're handing this over to God. He can take care of it. He has it covered.

There is nothing in the world you could do to make God love you more, and there's nothing in the world you could do to make God love you less. God loves you—not because of anything you could ever do, but because of Jesus. Because of what Jesus did for you, you're in good standing with God. He loves you, you have access to Him, and He wants a relationship with you—right this second, and forever. Take some time to reflect on that today.

Day 84

I don't know about you, but sometimes I can be cruel to myself—harsh, judgmental, unforgiving. Sometimes I look in the mirror, and all I can see are the ways I'm falling short. But thankfully that's not how God sees me. Take some time to talk to God about how you see yourself these days and ask Him to adjust your vision. Ask Him to help you see yourself the way He sees you. He will help you. I know He will.

Day 85

Take some time to pray for our world. Pray for people who are hungry, people who are thirsty, people who are hurting, people who are lonely, people who are displaced, and people who are in danger. Your prayer may feel like a small drop in a very big bucket, but God promises us that prayer is powerful and effective. So pray boldly today. Also—take a few minutes to brainstorm with God one way you could help.

What's something big and a little bit scary that you dream of doing, but are not sure you could find the courage to actually do? What if God told you that He'd be there every step of the way? Would that change things? Talk to him about it.

I believe that God created each one of us on purpose and for a purpose. What's one gift you know God has given you? Maybe you're artistic, or a beautiful singer, maybe you're a whiz at math or an amazing teacher. Maybe you're really kind, or a great listener. Maybe you have a passion for fighting the injustices of the world or a gift for making really great food. God put these things in us because He wants to use them. He wants us to use them to love His people, to take care of them right alongside Him. So what's one thing you know God has placed in you that He wants you to share with the world? Thank Him for that, and take a few minutes to think of one way you could share that gift this week.

How has God been showing up in your life lately? The more we look back and see God's faithfulness in our lives, the easier it is to remember that He's faithful the next time we really need Him. So take some time to reflect today.

Take some time this morning to tell God how much you love Him, to thank Him for who He is in your life.

Day 90

How has your relationship with God changed over the last 90 days? Reflect on where you were in your faith 90 days ago, and on what you've seen change, transform, and unfold as you've been spending more time with Him. Thank God for what He's done, and then pray a bold prayer and ask Him to take you deeper!

Stephanie May Wilson

is an author, blogger, speaker, and best friend who writes about the kinds of things you'd talk about at a girls' night at your best friends house: friendship, faith, relationships, and self-confidence. She says, "We're navigating life, and doing it together!"

You can join the conversation at StephanieMayWilson. com, or check out her first book, *The Lipstick Gospel*! It's her story of finding God in heartbreak, the Sistine Chapel, and the perfect cappuccino. You can also catch up with her on Instagram @smaywilson. She'd love to meet you!

Made in the USA
Monee, IL
12 October 2020